Dawn of the day

A POETRY ANTHOLOGY BY WINGLESS DREAMER

Edited by: Ruchi Acharya

Thank you so much for all your efforts and support that you gave to me in past few months. I'm very happy to receive the book as it is my first time when my poem got published and I want thought to show my gratitude to you through this mail. Hope we get to work together again in the future and wishing you all the best for future endeavours.- Mitali Prasad

I am already a follower of your Instagram and Facebook page, since December 2020 and find the contents thoroughly enjoyable.- Swarnadip Chatterjee

Hi there, I just wanted to say that after reading some of the poetry on Wingless Dreamer, I feel inspired and in awe. I've been writing on and off as a hobby for a few years now but seeing what you've done and how you've built this whole community of writers, I'm really inspired and impressed. You've given me just a bit more inspiration to keep working on my projects and for that I thank you.- Ryan

Best of afternoons! I am Arnaldo Batista, author of the poem "Hypochondriac Thriving," that your publication has chosen to enter in your "Fruits of our Quarantine" contest. I am simply sending this email to first thank you for this as I am truly humbled by your decision to accept this poem for publication. I wrote this poem after many nights of night terrors and panic attacks due to my looming anxiety over the pandemic and instant changes the world is going through seemingly overnight. Your validation of this poem is received by such validation and a feeling of triumph that I cannot put into words, so genuinely, thank you. -Arnaldo Batista

Proud and grateful to be included in one of your previous books. I will purchase and help promote your continued good work- J Brooke

It took me so long to get into reading & writing poetry, but last summer, I finally felt inspired to do it. In December 2019, I was published for the first time as a poet!! My poem is featured in the winter edition of Passionate Penholders by @winglessdreamerlit (available on Amazon) Poetry is always so relaxing to me and I hope that during this time of "unknowns," hopefully, we can all be inspired to relax a little and curl up with some good poetry! It's finally here!!! I am officially a published author check it out for yourself on Amazon! Thank you @winglessdreamerlit for believing in my work! – Landri Driskill

Keep up this excellent work. Poetry truly connects the readers with poetic souls across countries and cultures – Amita Sanghvi

It is a great joy for me that a kindhearted editor of a journal like you has liked my poem. Thank you again. I am hundred percent willing to publish my poem, "Oh beautiful beloved" in The book issue called Diversity: There's a beauty in that too. Be happy in life this is my heartfelt wishes to you.- Sandip Saha

I truly admire their creative publication who works so hard to promote emerging writers and artists for what they truly deserve and make them feel much appreciated. Hats off.- Josh Sullivan

Unlike traditional publisher Wingless Dreamer has supported and encouraged me to a great extent. -Sowmyata Singh

Dawn of the day poetry book

Wingless Dreamer

CULTURAL REGENERATION THROUGH OUR
CREATIVE COMMUNITY

Dawn of the day poetry book

DAWN OF THE DAY POETRY BOOK

Edited by

RUCHI ACHARYA

Wingless Dreamer

ABOUT US

The Wingless Dreamer Community was coined in 2015 by an Indian author Ruchi Acharya and was officially registered in 2019 to bridge the gap between emerging writers or artists and traditional publishing. Ruchi's community is a global platform for those who truly believe in themselves and are passionate about writing, art, and designing. It's the dream of her community to create a space where the authors or artists are free to express themselves.

Wingless Dreamer works with writers, artists, and designers to strengthen cultural regeneration, both in big cities and smaller towns across the globe. Our community has slowly but steadily grown with artists and writers from all over the world. Over time Wingless Dreamer became the main stage for well-known professional writers and artists to express themselves, all at the same place.

We envisioned a community where writers and artists would be invited to publish solely based on the merit of their writing and creative skills. The Wingless Dreamer community connects all essences of writing, illustrating, editing, marketing, and promoting on a single platform so that authors and illustrators don't have to go through the hardships of the publishing processes and focus on their work. The Community members become part of the family and are guided, supported, and encouraged on every step they make towards their writing and art career. The members can get access to free critiques, reviews, marketing, and in some cases funding for their work.

Our Wingless Dreamer team spends lots of time and energy creating as many contests as possible on different themes every quarter so that writers and artists can truly enjoy their experience with us.

The community is still growing and its accomplished authors and artists speak for themselves.

FOUNDER'S PEN

Being a writer can sometimes be solitary and quiet. A writer can understand how it feels to fall in love with every single character, battle with dialogues, work with vivid poetic devices, endeavor for perfection, and build an entire universe from scratch. Guess what? You're not alone. We understand the efforts you put every day into your work. Since we are a team of writers and artists too.

The art and writing industry is always considered as something obscure and profound by the public in general. It has become so difficult to stand alone and be noticed in the art industry or to stick with a writing career in the commercial society we live in today. Compared to other financial and economic-related jobs, things related to art are the minority.

Art and poetry are the most important elements of our life as it helps us understand and appreciate the world around us. No matter what anybody tells you words and ideas have the power to change the world and sneaks the truth upon you.

In the end, I would like to urge all the people who are reading this to never ever give up on your dreams. Seize the day. Every day counts. You're art. Never step back from showing your creative side to the world.

-Ruchi Acharya, Wingless Dreamer Founder

CONTENTS

S.NO	TITLE	AUTHOR	PAGE
1.	MAKE THE WORLD COME TO YOU	VALERIE SOPHER	15
2.	AUGUST AFTERNOON	KATRINA KAYE	17
3.	DEPRESSANT YOU ON WHEATBELT ROADS	SPENCER DAVIS	19
4.	PATHS OF MYSTERY	BREE LETO	21
5.	UNDULATING BEAUTY	PRATEEKSHA JOSHI	23
6.	THE MISSED OPPORTUNITY	V S BALAKRISHNAN	24
7.	SILVER SPLINTERS	OLIVIA LEE STOGNER	25
8.	POMAA	CHARLES YAW NYAME NEWTON	26
9.	THE RISE	TS S. FULK	28
10.	I SHOULD HAVE KNOWN	ANANIAS REESE	29
11.	HEAD ON MY LAP	LISA MOLINA	30
12.	AUBADE	MARGARET MARCUM	32

13.	AFTERNOON SHOWER	JUSTIN BYRNE	33
14.	THE LAST NIGHT	ANDY BETZ	34
15.	I DIE AT DAWN	MATEO PEREZ LARA	35
16.	AT DAWN	MEGAN LLOYD	36
17.	NOVELATI AND FAMILY INFANT FORMULA COMPANY	THOMAS OSATCHOFF	38
18.	MARCH ROSES	ANNA ZILBERMINTS	39
19.	BLESSED WITH THE MEMORIES OF THE PAST	CHEREZE SALOME BOOYSEN	41
20.	6.42 AM	LORRAINE HENRIE LINS	42
21.	TRANSCENDENCE	JENNIFER ETHERIDGE	43
22.	THE LAST MOMENT	STEVEN KISH	44
23.	TODAY	GRATIA SERPENTO	46
24.	THE SUN NEVER RISES	DALE SHANK	48
25.	THE PRIDE OF THE LION	NATALIE KORMOS	50
26.	WHEN ALL IS SUN	GAVIN BOURKE	52
27.	STOLEN MOMENT	JAMES B. NICOLA	53

28.	MOMENTS OF LIGHT	TRACEY DEAN WIDELITZ	54
29.	SENSORY TRAINING	SUZIE	55
30.	A WAY TO THE DAWN	TOSHIHISA NIKAIDO	57
31.	SUMMER SOLSTICE	DONALD GUADAGNI	58
32.	OH LEAVES AND GRASS	SKYLAR	60
33.	LIGHTS	SEDRIC AHLERS	63
34.	MY SKIN FEELS LIKE SPRING	THERESE POKORNEY	65
35.	DEADLOCKED	MEGAN LEMIEUX	66
36.	THE DAWN OF DAY	ARI CUBANGBANG	67
37.	THIS	NATALLI AMATO	68
38.	WHISPERING WILLOW	CALLEN HARTY	69
39.	8.10 AM AROUND THE MOORHEAD POOL	BRYNN TESKE	70
40.	DAWN	YUU IKEDA	72
41.	SILENCE OF SNOW	NICOLE FARMER	73
42.	A LOVE LETTER TO WHAT FOLLOWS	SYNA MAJUMDER	75

43.	LONG PRISTINE YARDS ALWAYS AHEAD	G. L NEWMAN	77
44.	THE TREES WAKE UP	MARY NEWCOMER	78
45.	PLAYGROUND	J.M. ALLEN	79
46.	IN THE COOL OF THE MORNING	ROD FRANCISCO	80
47.	IF YOU LISTEN	CHRISTA PLANKO	81
48.	RUST	EMMA WELLS	82
49.	ECHOES	CLIVE GRESSWELL	85
50.	A WALK AT DAWN	LUKE THOMAS SILLIMAN	86
51.	WE SAW THE FLOWERS YESTERDAY	JULIE CREASEY	88
52.	EARTH MORNING	DAN FITZGERALD	89
53.	THE GATES OF THE SKY	LILY ANDERSON	90

NEVER GIVE UP ON YOUR DREAMS. BE A WINGLESS DREAMER.

BELIEVE IN YOURSELF

I want to use this opportunity to thank all the participants, Wingless Dreamer team and community members to make this publication possible. Thank you for your support. More power to your pen.

Warm and kind regards,

Ruchi Acharya
Wingless Dreamer Founder

1. MAKE THE WORLD COME TO YOU

awake, thankful for what sleep came
in a night of unremembered dreams

brew amber assam in a porcelain teapot from London
on a good day, wonder when you will visit again

smooth covers on a made bed
semblance of control in an uncontrollable time

watch night's threads unravel into dawn
the imperceptible moment day becomes day

clouds catch colors of the cresting sun
shadows lengthen on east-facing houses

a jet breathes in clear cold air, exhales a bird tail
vapor trail, finches preen on bare branches

walkers tell the temperature in quilted jackets
and woolen caps, a terrier in a plaid vest

pick up your pen filled with ink the color of storm
wake up what is still asleep with words

tasting bittersweet like lost childhood wonders
a carousel of galloping painted ponies

you realize you are not watching
the sun rise, but the earth turn

words come until you reach bottom
turn the page and wonder

how will you fill this empty space?
how far will you walk for your story?

on this new sheltering day
make the world come to you

VALERIE SOPHER

Valerie Sopher found her poetic voice while sheltering in place. She is grateful to these journals for publishing her poems: Wingless Dreamer (Shakespeare of today), SLANT, Prometheus Dreaming, and Canary. She lives in the San Francisco Bay Area.

2. AUGUST AFTERNOON

We dance in
the heat of the kitchen.
Van Morrison plays lazily
from the living room,

me,
paper thin sun dress,
void of the undergarments
that would only cause
lines of sweat in already
wrinkled skin,
catching the breeze between
bare legs;

you,
with the grease still in
the creases of your hands,
holy jeans hanging low
on bare waist,
crooked smile plays
on parted lips;
we dance.

You would not take
no for an answer,
would not acknowledge
my casual stumble
over your bare feet,
toes somehow chilled
despite the summer heat.

We sway across kitchen
counters singing along
to every word,
hair sticking to temples,
mouth dry save for

the song on tongue.

You tell me I am
beautiful and, in that
rare delusion of August,
I believe you.

KATRINA KAYE

Katrina Kaye is a writer and educator living in Albuquerque, NM. She is seeking an audience for her ever-growing surplus of poetic meanderings. She hoards her published writing on her website: ironandsulfur.com. She is grateful to anyone who reads her work and is in awe of those willing to share it.

3. DEPRESSANT YOU ON WHEATBELT ROADS

Driving in the southwest heat
rising catatonically on tender slopes
away from town:
you left in rathe to beat the rush.

Strewn amongst their Milo cups -
sugar high evaporates -
like granite outcrops in the wheat
the kids asleep across the back.
Their pre-dawn sortie cannon-fire
arguments between them lulled -
it rests with them in earthing light.

You know you needn't hold a grudge
(*kids should do as kids will do…*).

The gravel murmur harmonies
unlikely to distort her sleep,
riding shotgun, uncoiling to
strike (*Calm… retreating now*);
no emails circling in thoughts
that break like aspirin in a glass.
More likely smooth, the skin behind,
sunnies shrouding corneas.

You know your wife (*Too proud to show…*).
A lapse! Look closer at her lips,
they gently disclose rhythmic sounds,
the same you count at midnight's bell.

Now time for your highway exhaust
mind diffuse in inselbergs;
they rise amongst the mildest slopes,
born anew in redden clay,
meet your muttered orisons,
shielded under slumber breath.

Windscreens crackreveal the sight:

echo kookaburras, they
rejoice (*We're heading south…*).

SPENCER DAVIS

Spencer Davis is an emerging Western Australian poet who works at a secondary private school as Head of English. His work has previously featured in Cottonmouth, TROVE, and The Vital Sparks, among other online publication spaces. He is currently interested in the impact of using parenthetical elements in poetry and counts Whitman, Auden, and Kingsolver as his primary influences.

4. PATHS OF MYSTERY

Walking upon paths of mystery
uncertain where we are going
daring to climb unexplored mountains
treading in territories we have never seen
around the bend
over that hill
traverse the lake
navigate the ridge
ever onwards
walking the paths
the paths of mystery

We may understand the terrain
a river is a river
a cave is a cave
but just like lovers
no two are the same
So, we remain trekking
seeking and searching
the unknown
the unknown paths

Aren't we only ever hunting
the salty border of the sea?
Without it we have no self-control
we'll keep exploring
keep discovering
keep pushing
walking ground down
down into paths

And once we reach that inevitable boundary
we will finally realise
the journey hasn't ended?
Instead, we will journey onwards
onto the boat

onto the afterlife
onto unmappable paths
the paths of mystery

BREE LETO

Bree Leto is an Australian poet who writes to connect with the hearts of people and give their secrets a voice. She has a propensity for whimsy, exploring hidden desires and buried emotions. Bree recently self-published her debuted poetry book, All Our Secrets and has been published in a number of anthologies and online literary journals including: League of Poets, Spillwords Press, Sad Girls Club Lit, City Limits Publishing, Poets' Choice and PureHaiku. Enjoy more of her work at www.secretthoughtswithin.com or on IG: @secretthoughtswithin

5. UNDULATING BEAUTY

The gods dropped glitter,
Amiss by inches from their art.
Chaotic, messy
But full of beauty.
And in those lights,
Like it rained stars instead,
Like the ocean sparkled under the sun,
Like the eyes of a distant lover,
Within my reach,
But beyond my grasp just the same.
Up close it is dazed and ugly,
But like all things filthy,
We're a dirty world,
Looking for beauty where lay none.
And I wish someone captures me in ink this moment,
As my heart rises and falls as tides do,
And I hope someone is looking at me,
Looking at me wonder,
And I am saved somewhere,
And my soul is embalmed.

PRATEEKSHA JOSHI

Prateeksha Joshi is an amateur writer from India. She majored in English Literature from the University of Delhi. She lives across the country and has a dog named Pudgy. She also loves singing and writing songs.

6. THE MISSED OPPORTUNITY

It's not even seven in the morning and the sun is burning bright.
The shape-shifting sand dunes that stretch for miles in every direction
Are moving to another location looking to claim their next victim.
My legs buried to the knees in the scorching ground
Plead to my own shadow for a momentary reprieve.
If not for my protective outer shell, I wouldn't have been able
To wait in this blistering heat in the middle of nowhere with open jaws
For that dewdrop to fall ultimately into my thirsty mouth sliding down the leaf.
And now is the moment… swish, the solitary plant swayed to the side
Right on time with the blowing wind, spilling the precious liquid
That took hours to accumulate on the porous ground which engulfed it
In no time right before my eyes. And you know what?
Life in the desert as a wandering beetle is no fun thing.

V S BALAKRISHNAN

V S Balakrishnan is a BA English graduate writing from Tamil Nadu, India. He is 30 years old. He is fond of writing poems right from his school days and he writes in both English and his mother-tongue Tamil, and has self-published a poetry chapbook in both. His works have appeared in Pif Magazine, Better than Starbucks Magazine, Plants and Poetry Journal, Poets Choice, Castello Duino Poesia, The Wire's Dream Magazine, Coffee People Zine, Unstamatic Magazine, and Dissident Voice. Besides writing, he is also interested in gardening and painting as well.

7. SILVER SPLINTERS

One star before the dawn goes out
falling shivers as I lie
a splinter of years
is covering me
drawing the quilts close up under
to catch this quiet cold.
I see shadows on the wall I long to be real—
but like falling asleep, it is not a choice;
it comes as it comes on soft feet, sometimes suddenly,
and the more I fight the more tired and awake I become.
I must let it ease into what it will be,
but there is no rest without these thoughts of you;
there is no rest for the dawn shattered night.
I hold my silver splinters in unfastened hands.
I watch their glow disappear with the dawn.

OLIVIA LEE STOGNER

Olivia Lee is a poet, novelist, playwright, and English professor. She has published two novels. Her poetry has been published by Writing for Peace-DoveTales, Sonnets for Shakespeare, Haunted Waters Press, Wild Roof Journal, Underwood Press, and the Closed Eye Open, among others. Her play, In Emma's Rendell Attic, had a pre-pandemic stage reading and was well received. She is committed to social justice work and supporting Fair Trade companies. She enjoys traveling, books, art, listening to music, walking in the woods, and spending time with her sister, Suzie, and their two dogs, George MacDonald and Keeper. Connect: instagram@ladyolivialee

8. POMAA

On that hill
Where knowledge stand
Did I see you.
Saw you in that huge hut
Where the doves of the sky perched
And the stallions of terrestrial space
Sat,squatted and stood
Just to listen to the wisdom
And knowledge of Solomon.
There you were seated.
Yes!Seated at the last corner
Of that wooden bench
Waiting patiently like the bee
For a flower to suck your nectar.
When I saw you,
Even in the dead-raising noise
That could shame a sparrow haven,
I heard the thump beat of my heart.
There you were with your hair,
As dark as the soot
That baths my mother' s pot.
Flowing like the Livingstone Falls,
Falling from the Fountains of Frank-burg
Into the sea of Siberia,at the
Southern sector of the sand dunes.
Your appearance brightened my face
As the heavenly diamonds show
Every secret deer' s path.
Your eyes shone like those
Of the mother of ages
Which caused the first stallion to abandon
The So-Ancient.
Your lips called for a hot wow.
When the clouds gathered like a swamp of locusts
About to attack a corn field,
The little bird in flight was waiting.

Even as a red-eyed lion,
Looking for a prey.

CHARLES YAW NYAME

Charles Yaw Nyame Newton is a TEFL teacher who enjoys writing screenplays, short stories and poetry. When he's not writing, he's probably playing the piano.

9. THE RISE

Jet black darkness, the moonless sky's
patiently waiting for the sun
to scare away the absence of
color, brightness, and all things good
it's just an orb of gas and heat
yet the sight of this yellow ball
over the horizon can cause
oratorios in the throats
of bird and man alike
the symphony of dawn
as conducted by God
for the hearing of both
angel and man alike
all of the planets sing
Is it really a surprise that
I rejoice to greet her

TS S. FULK

TS S. Fulk lives with his wife and three children in Örebro, Sweden as an English teacher and textbook author. After getting an M.A. in English literature from the University of Toronto, he taught in Prague, CZ before settling down in Sweden. Besides teaching and writing, TS S. Fulk is an active musician playing bass trombone, the Appalachian mountain dulcimer and the Swedish bumblebee dulcimer (hummel). His poetry has appeared in the book Snowdrops by Wingless Dreamer.

10. I SHOULD HAVE KNOWN

I should have known from the absence of rain
Or the humming birds singing in the horizon
That the moment you left me in your rearview
I should have been thanking you

I should have known from the sun, the way it shined down on me
The way the subtle breeze dried my tears as I watched you leave
How the sky was clear and blue as I drove home alone after you left my view
I had a frown that should've been a smile but I didn't have a clue
I should have been thanking you

I should have known from the pollen at the birth of a new spring
That I survived the loneliness of September
And endured the cold everlasting loss of December
But how was I supposed to know that I'd meet the greatest love of my life in June
Now that I look back on it, I should have been thanking you

I should have known from the rain and the cloudy grey skies
That something was different the moment I saw her pure sapphire eyes
It was a perfect storm that corrected all of my emotions
That lead me to a never before seen perfect shade of blue
And for that I'm thanking you.

ANANIAS REESE

Ananias Reese; Born November 30, 1992 is an American writer/poet who spends most of his time writing about the beauty of the world as well as the horrors. His work is inspired by painful heartbreaks as well as the hope of a true unbreakable love.

11. HEAD ON MY LAP

I place my head
upon my lap,
so I may
sit just
here
and
now.

No past regrets.
No future frets.

Just
sitting
gently
cradling
my
thoughts

as a newborn babe
bathing in the comforts
of sweet air, dirt,
and leaves;

And leaning safely into
my womb of peace.

LISA MOLINA

Lisa Molina is a writer/educator in Austin, Texas. She has taught high school English and Theatre Arts, and later served as Associate Publisher of Austin Family Magazine. Molina now works with students with special needs. She has twice been chosen as a winner of the Beyond Words Magazine "250-Word Creative Challenge," and was chosen as "Poet of the Week" on the Instagram page of The Literatus for her haiku sonnet "Thinking of Sylvia" during its National Poetry Month celebration. Molina's writing can also be found in numerous journals, including Wingless Dreamer, The Ekphrastic Review, Trouvaille Review, Neologism Poetry Journal, Fahmidan Journal, The Daily Drunk, and Amethyst Review.

12. AUBADE

Daybreak cries inside and I
    by design
in congruence remember.

Moon's silver liquor
cradles the mist of
midnight. A pale moment
glimmers the rain of suppression.

Mirror of flames envelop the last straws
of reason undefeated.
Doves soar from the scars embedded
on white walls.

I begin against the sand spilling
into your chest. The chirping clock tells me:
the tornado is rising, so I paddle
incorrigible and alone. Shining violet
clouds move closer to my magenta heart.

The lemon sun laughs
    in an order
yellow with eager.

MARGARET MARCUM

Margaret Marcum is currently a third-year graduate student in the MFA Program in Creative Writing at Florida Atlantic University in Boca Raton. She graduated with a BA (emphasis on poetry) from the University of Redlands, where she was a member of the Proudian Interdisciplinary Honors Program. Her literary interests include ecofeminism and healing the collective through personal narrative. She has published poems in Children, Churches, and Daddies, Amethyst Review, Writing in a Woman's Voice, and Flora Fiction. And she was a finalist for the 2021 Rash Award in Poetry sponsored by Broad River Review.

13. AFTERNOON SHOWER

Afternoon Shower
Dripping against the window with a
Natural syncopation.
Hiding the blue behind a veil of gray.

The ground is coated in water to
Entice sporadic rainbows
To display their kaleidoscopic array.

Sunlight dances in the distance with
Contagious motivation;
Bookending the intermission of rainfall.

As soon as it began, it ended, like a
Child's nursery story.
Nature's break in daily monotony
.

JUSTIN BYRNE

Justin Byrne is an elementary teacher in Middle Tennessee. Justin earned his bachelor's degree in Elementary Education with dual minors of Music and English from Middle Tennessee State University. Justin's work can also be seen in Plants & Poetry, multiple books by Poets' Choice, The Parliament Literary Magazine, multiple books by Wingless Dreamer, The Thing Itself, Shift: A MTSU Write Publication, and Brick Street Poetry. Justin can be found on his website byrnepoetry.com.

14. THE LAST NIGHT

He insisted and never wavered
She resisted, no party favor
Under the gaslight on dock sixteen

His decision and he told her so
Complete derision as she said no
She was too young to wed a marine

He would ship out, in the morn at dawn
She could pout, but to him she was drawn
Despite all the dangers left unseen

The metronome timed meeting misses
In catacombs of fleeting kisses
One lost love never to reconvene

ANDY BETZ

Andy Betz has tutored and taught in excess of 40 years. He lives in 1974, and has been married for 29 years. His works are found everywhere a search engine operates.

15. I DIE AT DAWN

with the rod still protruding from my heart
sickly copper, gagging gold, still glistening and humming dazzle
if you read this, hear my body bare its weight of aftermath, listen
I want gowns, makeup, lightning strikes to my blackened wood
casket: bury it under a dense forest, pick anywhere, and play Purity Ring
then dance, then make phantoms welcome
make blood, stiffen happy, be kind to the charge, let it swallow
fill of nourishment:
nothing fancy, let the rot
swell into bloom
into vast, superior glory.

MATEO PEREZ LARA

Mateo Perez Lara is a queer, non-binary, Latinx poet from California. They received their M.F.A. in Poetry as part of the first cohort to graduate from Randolph College's Creative Writing Program. They are an editor for RabidOak Online Literary Journal. They have a chapbook, Glitter Gods, published with Thirty West Publishing House. Their poems have been published in EOAGH, The Maine Review, and elsewhere.

16. AT DAWN
For Sora Marie

all night long, you have slept in my arms
I breathe easier, sticky with your sweat

breath comes easy now, sticky and sweaty
once, I woke at dawn and bled, dreamlike

I once woke from a dawn dream, bleeding
the window: out on trees, in on this life, mine

my life looks out on trees; look in the window
this cup overflowing, so long parched, we drink

thirsty, we drink from this overflowing cup
each day, victory. years? miraculous.

each day a victory; years are miracles
I watched your first cells expand and grow

more than I can count now, expanding, growing
all night long, you have slept in my arms

with gratitude to Jericho Brown

MEGAN LLOYD

Megan Lloyd Joiner is a health care chaplain and the mother of two daughters. You can find her at www.revmeganlloydjoiner.org.

17. NOVELATI AND FAMILY INFANT FORMULA COMPANY

Singular sunrise or sunset. Let's go surfing early.
Tribe or trip: leave the other goats to themselves.
They can go down to the coconut river,
eat the grass and their own hapax legomenon
shade under mangosteens

stretching red-violet hair
highlights transmitting Hypatia's parturient
waterfall picnic, bulawan. Mangosteens
love to hear our nonce songs. Oval ◎ leaves
our boats ⤴ or birds with blades for wings.
Let's get buko juice, we're thirsty.
Buko juice for Bugoy's thirsty, too.
Bugoy can carry the buko....
Bugoy knows the way....Who can open it?
Once said machete to get it all back
in just one swipe. Day's opening darkness star patterned cape
projecting patience into our body waves
the machete moon

swipes to see waterfall gloam.
Look for us—we'll be gone casa right here.
Yerba mate growing in the break-
down c'mon ba-ba ga-ga,
what's the nascent group of all of us called?

THOMAS OSATCHOFF

Thomas Osatchoff, together with family, is building a self-sustaining home near a waterfall. Recent work has appeared in Acorn Review Literary Journal, scissors & spackle, WinglessDreamer, and elsewhere.

18. MARCH ROSES

I found the end
of the sidewalk. It's nothing
spectacular, it's nothing
the stories prepared
me for. A rose garden stretches out
ahead of me, and I want to say
something cliché about
it, but I'm not very
good at this.
I'll try to carry
out what I promised, but
god forbid (or God forbid?)
I lose the pace and just
stand there, so you know
where to find me
if I'm
lost.

ANNA ZILBERMINTS

Anna Zilbermints is a graduate of the University of Iowa in English and psychology. She also does spoken word, participating in local slams, and having a video posted on Button Poetry's page.

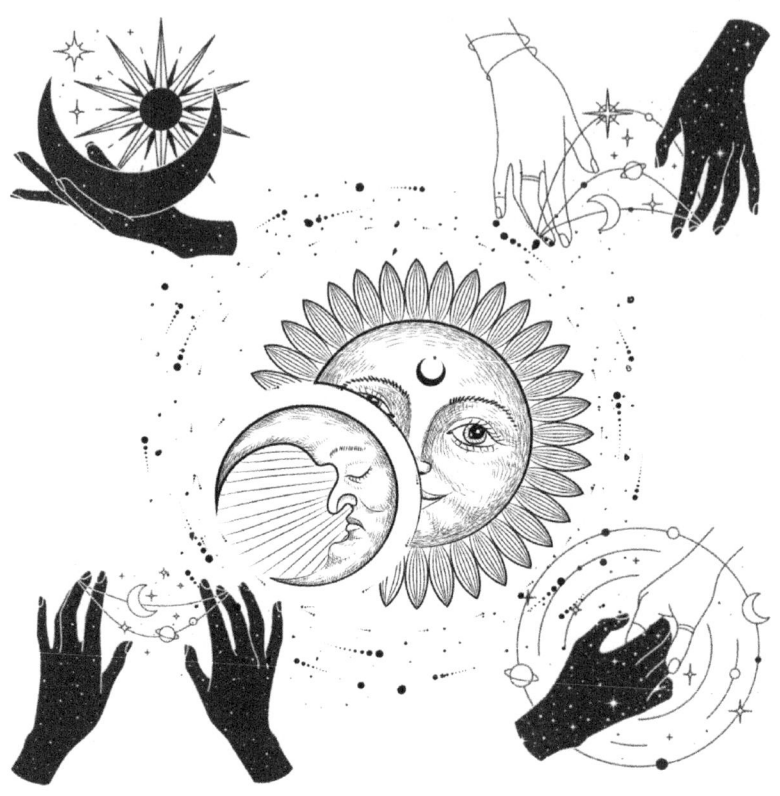

19. BLESSED WITH THE MEMORIES OF THE PAST
(Tribute Uncle Barry & Uncle Derek Williams)

The dawn of a new future
The old leaves of the past
Brown with the harshness of winter
With the bold pilgrims of soothing air
Living waters and the caress of the wind
My soul swept up its eyelashes
Rested at the dimples of life
Deep with contempt and hurt
Deep with a longing for a life that never again can be again
The mornings of Christmas
Just to be together would be enough
The bond of a once perfect family
Disappeared like mist fading in the sun
The past was our best, our most treasured time
An era of not being rich,
An era of clarity, belonging, trust
Where time was everything and jokes our forte
With laughter and hugs and kisses ...
I will never forget you.

CHEREZE SALOME BOOYSEN

Chereze Salome Booysen published her first poem in a chapbook at age of 17 years old. She continued publishing in two more chapbooks. She competed in a National Hermes Olympiad Essay Competition, where she scored two A's in grade 11 and in grade 12. She matriculated in 2006. She studied Journalism for six months online course through the University of Zululand. Which was extended to 12 after contracting tuberculosis. While her classmates moved on graduating, Chereze Booysen, was in the hospital during the final exam in 2007. She completed the course, while on TB treatment. She, however, received her Journalism Diploma through the mail. In the year 2010, Chereze , got the opportunity to study at City Varsity, in Johannesburg for two years. She studied and completed a course in Film and Television Production Techniques graduating in 2012. Chereze reverted back to her first love, writing poetry.

20. 6.42 A.M.

Even in the dark cold of January,
with windows drawn up tight,
I honor the the fump-a-thump
of music spilling down the roadway,

the chew of beat becoming more urgent
as it approaches, the bizzzz of hood and trunk
chattering on the back beat, drowning out the gossip
of tires on asphalt, low graveled hum of engine—

knowing damn well, someone
in that car is either having the best
moment of their week
or sharing a very private rage.

LORRAINE HENRIE LINS

A little bit about me? I am a Pennsylvania county Poet Laureate and author of four books of poetry. I serve as the Director of New and Emerging Poets with Tekpoet and am a founding member of the "No River Twice" improvisational poetry troupe. My work has appeared in a wide collection of publications, and a small graffiti poster in New Zealand. Born and raised in the suburbs of Central New Jersey, this self-professed Jersey Girl now resides along the coast of Carolina where she has learned to pump her own gas. Please visit my website: www.LorraineHenrieLins.com for more information

21. TRANSCENDENCE

Finding peace through transcendence,
My focus, on nature's joy...
Instead of pain or vengeance,
So, my soul, is not destroyed...
Outside of the pain and the loss,
Of sleepless nights and long days...
Feeling love, is too high a cost,
Leaving me lost, hurt and dazed...
My soul knows its mate is gone,
And, no other, will take the place...
And the pain, felt to my bones,
So, transcendence is my only grace...
Praying to overcome it all,
But, moving on, is not my plan...
Only once, in my life, I fall,
In love and now, desolate land...
Finding peace through transcendence,
Is my ultimate goal for now...
Needing peace, in its true essence,
Trying to find the what and how.

JENNIFER ETHERIDGE

Jennifer Etheridge is an expressionist at heart. She loves to write poetry and short stories. Living in the woods, she is inspired by the peace and tranquility. She has lived enough for seven lifetimes, and wants to share her love for passion and her experience through poetry.

22. THE LAST MOMENT

I'm living my life minute by minute.
I can't live the cliché "take life day by day"; that's just too long.
The ticking clock in the living room is a consent reminder of my life slipping away.
Everyone has abandoned me; it's just me, the mirror, and the Grim Reaper lurking in the
background.
Looking at my reflection, I question myself; Did I push people away?
Am I my own worst enemy?
Or am I a victim?
Does it really matter which one it is?
The cold reality is I am loved but never want to be seen.
I only exist to put my family's mind at ease; leaving the Earth would cause them horrific pain.
The ticking of the clock turns into a metronome.
Tick...Tick...Tick...100 BPS.
It is driving me insane!
I can't take this noise and isolation!
The Grim Reaper turns up the metronome.
Tick..Tick..Tick..Tick..Tick.. and he starts to whisper in my ear.
He speaks softly about the journey to the afterlife and the freedom of letting go.
I scream, "No! I will not"!
He cranks up the metronome even faster; the living room is alive with the sounds of
woodpeckers.
"Don't live for others," as the Reaper keeps poisoning my thoughts.
This is some kind of trick as I yell into the emptiness.
The phone provides no help as loved ones blocked my calls.
Insomnia has taken over; I can't sleep because the Reaper killed the Sandman.
I can't live like this!
Ideas whirl around in my head: take a walk, get a gun, call mom, get some rope.
The Reaper rubs my shoulder's lulling me into his submission.
My idle hands start to make a hangman's noose.

"Stop, this isn't right"! But there is no one to prevent me from manipulating the rope.
Ha ha ha! A sinister chuckle runs up my spin.
My hands slip on the noose like grandma putting on her pearl neckless; oh, how I miss her so.
The rope feels like bliss around my neck, or at least that's what the Reaper is telling me.
The fibers of the rope fill my nostrils. Is this my last smell of this world?
The rope tightens around my neck.
It's my last hug. The embrace is so tight.
A rush of heat fills my depressed body.
Sounds disappear, lights flicker, and blackness becomes permanent.
Is this my last moment in life?
Snap! The rope breaks.
Gasping for air, realizing what I have done, I yell out "thank you" to an empty house.

STEVEN KISH

Steven Kish is a writer who lives in Las Vegas, Nevada. He has endured childhood trauma, and is a survivor of suicide. His writing shows what life is like, when someone is living on the edge of madness/sorrow. The poet is always trying to describe what cannot be said. When Steve shared his writing with the public, it was received with positivity and people confirming that they too hurt, but were unwilling to "put themselves out there", but people found comfort that he was hurting, just like them. Steven's poems have been published in, on-line journals such as: Continue the Voice (Issue 7 & 8, UK). The Elevation Review (Issue 5, USA), and The Rainbow Poems Review (Issue 4, UK) He is currently getting published in Pure Slush Books (Lifespan Vol 3 & 4 AU). He also has three poems being released in Night Picnic Press (EN, RU) later this year.

23. TODAY

Yesterdays are old and cold
Gone
We lived them
Lied, cried, bribed
Terrible humans we were

But the sun
The sun as it crests over the hilltop
Sending light through tree tops and
Over berry shrubs
A message attached to a ray

Yesterday was failed
Tomorrow is unsure
But Today
Today is a chance of a lifetime
A day to be reborn

A day where we
Will not have to lie
Cheat
Steal
With pettiness and greed

Today is a day where
Forgiveness is plausible
Where we can right Yesterday's wrong
Survival was the first step
Living is the final

Golden glows and golden rules
We shall honor
We shall pray
We have mend
All for Today.

GRATIA SERPENTO

Gratia Serpento is an Oregonian poet/journalist with a mild root beer obsession. She's had works published in Poor Yorick, not a type Magazine, Poetry Nation, The Frost Place, Crystal Crush Magazine, Ishvara Wellness, Wingless Dreamer, among others. She loves to read, write, and avoid her problems. Check out her Instagram (@poet_serpento) to see previous/upcoming publications, exclusive poems, and pictures of her dog, Bernie Ernie.

24. THE SUN NEVER RISES

It's a meager gesture.
A nod to the geocentric lie
we were taught, and that still reigns.

Every morning as the night turns to daylight
I face east,
leaning backwards
for several moments.

Every evening as dusk turns to darkness
I face west,
leaning forwards
for several moments.

Homages to the fact
that the earth rotates on its axis
and that the sun does not rise
and that the sun does not set.

I lean against the direction of rotation
as though centrifugal force might tip me over.
It never does.
But I sunder the lingua franca
that still, unwittingly,
fuels the arrogance that the earth
is the center of our solar system.

Shame.

DALE SHANK

Dale Shank's fiction and poetry have been published in: Sterling Clack Clack, Wingless Dreamer, Exquisite Corpse, The Healing Muse, The Raw Art Review, Akros Review, Before the Sun, Croton Review, Joint Endeavor, Powder, and University of Portland Review.

25. THE PRIDE OF THE LION

Across the vast Savannah, before the sun has risen,
The baboon sits patiently on a rock, seeming to have such great wisdom.

The sky above begins to lighten, as a watercolour painting,
As if the blackened ink of night, from the morning sky is draining.

In the trees birds of every colour, alight from the branches with a joyful song,
Each animal takes its place, for many years in the place where he belongs.

Against the soft canvas of morning, the silhouettes of giraffes are painted,
Stretching their necks up high to leaves, in the air that remains untainted.

A Howler monkey in the far off jungle, screams his echoing good morning,
Warming his strong vocal chords, as if he were performing.

Zebra gallop across the sand, and circle around to splash through the stream,
Elephants slurp up water and spray, their wrinkly skin beginning to gleam.

The pearls of cool water drip from their backs, and splash melodiously into the river,
Sending out continuous ripples, the surface broken trembling with a quiver.

The sky now bursting into a symphony of colour, gives way to the rising sun,
A burning sliver emerges from the horizon, activity on the Savannah has long since begun.

Piercing the sky with rays of light, shining out in all directions,
Even through the darkness of night, in the morning the sun achieves such perfection.

Rising quite fast now into the sky, illuminating all stretches of the Earth,
Into the sunrise the eager birds, flit, swoop and fly forth.

Insects hum in the coming heat, which scorches the Savannah sand,
Yet in this burning sun its heat, the animals can withstand.

Among this tranquility and peaceful beauty, there lies the mighty king,
Yet as magnificent as he is, he has neither feathers nor wing.

Quietly he sits taking in the view, of his kingdom shared with all,
Each grain of sand and smallest bug, and trees so very tall.

The kiss of the rising sun, glistens through his golden mane,

As he peacefully watches life around him, on this magnificent, untouched plane.

And with all this beauty surrounding him, on this young day that is nigh,
The lion gazes above him, and gives a gentle sigh.

NATALIE KORMOS

A 2020 graduate of University of St Andrews, Scotland (Biology BSc), Natalie competes on the horse polo and ballroom dancing teams in addition to taking part in golf, sailing and reeling. Natalie began writing poetry when her mum read Hailstones and Halibut Bones to her at a very young age. Natalie's work has been featured in North American and Canadian poetry competitions hosted by Creative Communication, The Poetry Institute of Canada, The Royal Canadian Legion and Polar Expressions Publishing. Natalie has been featured in The Parliament Literary Journal's inaugural issue as the Ekphrastic poetry competition's Artist's Choice winner. Most recently her work 'Implosion', has been published in the summer issue of The Parliament Literary Journal. Natalie has a great passion in writing to share messages in a rhyming form for all ages, that challenge perspectives, inspire innovation and allow for creativity.

26. WHEN ALL IS SUN

Breathing, taking it all in on a scorching hot summer's day,
lying on grass surrounded by flowers,
of different kinds and varieties,
the heat, the scent, the sound of a stream close by
and a couple of bees and the clearest blue sky,
casting its wonderfulness all over the scene,
far removed today from an ordinary day.

Waited so long for a day like this feels almost like a dream,
time being beyond precious in such rare weather,
so caught up in the moments,
the trickling water, the cloudless blue sky,
the airplane trails, the sun baking, the green grass,
giving a year's heat and light in just a few random hours,
enough to cure the whole world of any unhappiness,
whatsoever and create world peace in a matter of seconds.

What more could anyone need than this blistering sunshine,
penetrating deep into our chemistries,
healing all wounds,
bright streaming, beams of warm silk finely spun,
around the seconds, minutes and hours,
when all is well, all is good, all is kind,
all is sun.

GAVIN BOURKE

Gavin Bourke grew up in the suburb of Tallaght in West Dublin. Married to Annemarie living in County Meath, he holds a B.A. in Humanities from Dublin City University, an M.A. Degree in Modern Drama Studies and a Higher Diploma in Information Studies from University College Dublin. He is widely published.

27. STOLEN MOMENT

A moment stolen as a jewel of calm
can host a new thought to repair the world

The eye of a hurricane cannot quite see
but I standing still and quiet midst storm swirls

have closed my eyes once or twice and seen all

.

JAMES B. NICOLA

> James B. Nicola, a returning contributor, is the author of six collections of poetry, the latest being Fires of Heaven: Poems of Faith and Sense. His decades of working in the theater culminated in the nonfiction book Playing the Audience: The Practical Guide to Live Performance, which won a Choice award.

28. MOMENTS OF LIGHT

I close my eyes, soaking in
warm rays of unfiltered sunshine, reflecting
all my yesterdays that will never return-
light pierces through my closed
lids feeling all its power in
this single moment that will soon be
another yesterday-
nobody is guaranteed a tomorrow,
for time eventually takes us all-
I will become one with today's shining
moment and make my future
unforgettable yesterdays.

TRACEY DEAN WIDELITZ

Tracey Dean Widelitz is an emerging poet. Her poetry has been published in Wingless Dreamer's 'Dreamstones of Summer' anthology, and she was the Grand Winner of Wingless Dreamer's 'Dreamstones of Summer' Poetry Contest. She sought a BA degree in English Literature, but Life had alternate plans in mind. Tracey is an emerging poet and photographer, and is the author of 'A Heavenly World', an upcoming published children's book. She enjoys her morning cinnamon tea and can't live without puppy kisses. You can visit her website at https://www.traceydeanwidelitz.com/

29. SENSORY TRAINING

If you are Paul with the brown eyes
how could you have taught me to write on my tongue   with parts of me
I had never possessed
Long ways and short ways
in waves
Describe the smells of an amusement park-
someplace you think we'll go-
 I'm terrified of heights.
How can I describe this exercise
 when your eyelashes are so long
  when your shoulders exist
   when your 5 o'clock shadow can brush-burn my thigh in a delicious
heat
 like pins in my solitude
If I don't wear a bra would you notice?
If I put on hot cocoa lip gloss
would you remember   as a boy unhinged
In that place I need you to be
 torn, clutching and sore
like my lips and my wrists
and the black and blue in my chest
If I hung from my ankles, serpentine at your side-
 while you hesitate and tear through my inner ear
 in
    a
      tomb
of heedless white noise

SUZIE

Suzie (she/her) is a self-taught poet who has made a full-time career of cataloging and tech services at a midsize public library. Her poem, "Holes" was published in the winter 2020 issue of Storm Cellar magazine. You can find her on Twitter @RedUp82.

30. A WAY TO THE DAWN

Here lies I, a truth be told,
Gone away, so few years old.
My words are etched in hearts,
Not etched in stone or left in arts.
Into nothingness,
we are all drawn,
But still,
we seek a way to the dawn

TOSHIHISA NIKAODO

Toshihisa Nikaido has worked on popular video game series such as Resident Evil, Pokémon, and The Legend of Zelda, and was one of the writers on a Zelda spinoff. Toshihisa more recently joined Japan's space exploration agency for a completely new challenge while using various forms of fiction writing as a creative outlet and has since been published in several literary journals.

31. SUMMER SOLSTICE

Night skies chasing scorpions and swans in flight, the music of the lyra drifts amongst
cirrus clouds accompanying northern mockingbirds from dusk to dawn, crickets songs wax and wane
in the warm summer night air.
The hue and awakening of the eastern sky, and the coo and call of the morning doves
herald the new day. There is a stillness in the air, a moment when the dew on the grass twinkles and the
soft rush of warm morning air touches and lifts the dew back into the waiting skies. The bats retreat to
their roosts and the swifts awaken to take their place.
The morning glories awake and the dandelions stir, the former will hide from the
summer heat and the latter will spread wide to embrace the full measure of the summer day. Shimmers
and waves of heat dance in the distance, ripples on the horizon that mock the rising sun as a mirage of
lenticular shapes.
Dragonflies warm and wake to patrol the ponds and lakeshores, honey and bumblebees hum
and seek the open blossoms of the early morning before the heat of the afternoon sets in to rule the
day. The zenith is near and the morning shadows grow short and disappear, grasshoppers jump from
sun to shade as sparrows pursue them until caught or evade.
Afternoon sets in with striking blue skies, cumulus clouds appear and then vanish
like magic, soft and white, billow and strain to grow, then evaporate before they truly begin. Languid air
holds as a long breath before dust devils begin to dance and disappear, a hawk's cry carries far as it rides
the afternoon thermals across the sky.
Softer winds caress the lands as dusk approaches, the cicada's song echoes in the trees.

The twilight settles over the skies and lightning bugs begin their
evening mating dance. Small
momentary lights as the cooling summer breeze touches the grass
ending the summer solstice dance

DONALD GUADAGNI

> Donald Guadagni is an international educator, author, and writer currently teaching and conducting research in Beijing China. His publication work includes fiction, non-fiction, poetry, prose, academic, photography and his artwork. Former iterations, military, law enforcement, prisons, engineering, and wayward son.

32. OH LEAVES AND GRASS

Lying out on the grass
dressed in shimmering green
and I can't help wondering
whatever happened to me
and how could it be
that I feel this serene?

The universe is holding me
grounding me
lulling me
rocking me to sleep
as the sun beats down upon me.
The anxious thoughts, they just pass by like the few clouds above.
Now I can't doubt that I've always been loved, always been taken care of.

Today reminds me of those old, faded books from high school--
what was it the women were talking about? Michelangelo?
I think so, and I think of all the things I used to feel:
these different sensations. A peach, maybe
tingling against my tongue, flattening against my teeth.
Hazelnut chocolate, shimmering against my taste buds.
Pure pleasure, pure sun.

And all the things I believed:
the things the greats said, and they gave me goosebumps
so they had to be right.
Every woman on earth was my sister, every man my brother
and some of both my lovers.
Yes, I truly believed this--
I still
believe it
and deep within my soul, I feel it.
The intrusiveness of my thoughts makes all beauty feel untrue
but not today. Not right now, anyway.

So what's happening to me?
There's a tightness in my chest almost all the time
but just for once I feel loose, languid, warm.
Somehow free.
You know, what I used to be best at was feeling free
not being free, but feeling
which was enough-- the feeling was what I believed.

And it's funny, because I really used to live in summer dresses.
Short and pink and tight and flowered and slitted--
so today, for old times' sake I decided to wear one
nice and tight, with a cut-out in each side.

Laying out on the grass again
later in the afternoon this time
and once more I can't help wondering:
whatever has happened to me
and how could it be
that after a morning of feeling so serene
I'm once again a ball of anxiety.

Lying with my lover under the cherry blossom trees--
my perfect, perfect lover. His skin is smooth, freshly shaven
he smells like lemongrass and the outdoors
even today, his shirt is collared and all I want is to inhale him.
He came to me upon a dream.
I'm trying to sleep while he reads, but I can't
because my mind is going ten million miles per hour
even as the sun beats down on me.

Nobody truly looks at each other anymore. I miss the outlines of faces.

What happened to us?
Masked girls across the field
are taking semi-pointless selfies.
I'm fighting off a panic attack and losing
because I forgot to pack hand sanitizer.
Every negative feeling I've ever had now threatens to overwhelm me.

Laying out on the grass
dressed in shimmering green.
I realize now, nothing ever really did happen to me.
I was born with an immeasurable fear
that lives and breathes inside me
and I live for the moments when I manage to feel serene.
I grip this feeling in my fingertips
pray for, wait for, and dream of
a day when it lasts longer than one heavenly, heavenly morning

SKYLAR

Currently Skylar is a nanny and private English tutor. She has been passionate about writing and poetry for years, and have had a couple of poems published in small anthologies.

33. LIGHTS

Lights, lights
Some are white
Some blue
All black at the end

Clouds, clouds
They rise
They fall

Well, well
Underground
There is water
And a hell

Nightmares
Either warn
Or tease

Heart, heart
Fight each other
Until they don't

On and on
Turn and nibble here
Next you find
What was before

Friends, friends
Up the street
Goodbye
You have an appointment

SEDRIC AHLERS

Sedric Ahlers is a poet with a brain injury from Duluth Minnesota. His style is hard, truthful, and from the heart. He likes to dive but he doesn't get wet. Sedric enjoys fishing, adrenaline, and Hyperbaric Oxygen Therapy.

34. MY SKIN FEELS LIKE SPRING

i went someplace in my dream last night;
someplace with a pink sky and an ocean

when i said you were beautiful this is what i meant

i backpacked around countries with strangers;
strangers with kind eyes and dirty fingernails

when i said you were beautiful this is what i meant

then i saw my sister give birth in august
and i'd give anything to be called this type of beautiful

you told me my eyes were so
blue
i know
what color they are

don't tell me my eyes remind you of the sea
tell me they look like winter
tell me my skin feels like spring

don't tell me i take your breath away
tell me i'm a fresh heartbeat
tell me i'm summer

THERESE POKORNEY

Therese is an amateur poet and writer who currently lives in Fairbanks, Alaska. Her works have been published in Not Very Quiet and Wingless Dreamer's "Heartfelt Poetry Collection."

35. DEADLOCKED

Half drunk on the mist,
Nestled sweetly below the tree line.
We exist in the calm between storms,
quiet moments, like raindrops hung from the
petals of a goldenrod,
Awaiting chaos.

The air is heavy with it,
Unspoken grief,
Sky still dark from its passing.
I tend the garden while I can,
No telling how much danger is held
Against the sky until it breaks itself open.

MEGAN LEMIEUX

Megan Lemieux is a full time biology student whose love of poetry often distracts her from her studies. She is currently unpublished, but hopes to continue to pursue her interest in writing and art.

36. THE DAWN OF DAY

The dawn of day breaks way the night.
Sun reaching through crack of sheets sheathing windows pain.
Day a new, moments of peace to be sought.
Turning over, rustling under neath the window sill.
Coffee beans, aroma filled, cold, crisp, air.

Wild life stirs at mornings light,
Frost tickles the noses of creatures linger.
Dull grey sky, broken open by winters snow.
Light fluff trickles down from the heavens.

Open door, coffee stowed in hand.
Peering through the lush, frostbitten yard.
Past the brush,
A female bear, deposits herself into her keep.
She shall slumber deep.
To hibernate, to not stir, nor wake until spring does break.

ARI CUBANGBANG

A University Student cultivating writing skills and creating political art with messages that aim to change social perceptions. I am an immunosuppressed woman; I have been stuck inside for nearly a year besides going to the doctor since COVID19. Art and writing are my main focuses. I am a fighter, someone who is continuing to go after their dreams regardless of the challenges that arise. I have am being published in a mental health anthology with Quillkeepers' Press.

37. THIS

It came and went -
first the sunset
then - aha! - our love
was like that.

But there is one other truth
that I do know and it is –

I shall have my dawn.

NATALLI AMATO

Natalli Amato is a poet, fiction writer, and journalist from upstate New York. She is the author of the poetry collection On a Windless Night and Burning Barrel (forthcoming from Finishing Line Press). Natalli was awarded the Edwin T. Whiffen Poetry Prize as an undergraduate at Syracuse University. Her poetry is deeply inspired by the North Country region of New York State where she grew up and continues to be drawn to. Her poetry has appeared in several anthologies and numerous literary publications, and she is a poetry reader for Carve Magazine. Outside of poetry, Natalli has covered music, lifestyle, and entertainment for Rolling Stone. She is currently working on her first novel. She lives in Sackets Harbor, New York.

38. WHISPERING WILLOW

Wind whips through the whispering willow
overlooking the crying, drying, dying
stream. She bows down in prayer,
gently sweeping over the banks,
giving thanks for her years of life
and the water that sustained her.

CALLEN HARTY

Callen Harty is the author of 24 produced plays, eight books, and countless essays and poems that have been published in various newspapers, magazines, and online sites around the country. His monologues for the Wisconsin Veterans Museum's annual cemetery tour, Talking Spirits, won awards from the Wisconsin Historical Society and the American Association of State and Local History. He wrote the program its first six years. He is a member of the Wisconsin Writers Association, Council for Wisconsin Writers, and the Wisconsin Fellowship of Poets. Originally from Shullsburg, Wisconsin, he now lives in Monona, Wisconsin with his partner, Brian, and several pets.

39. 8.10 AM AROUND THE MOORHEAD POOL

At 8:10am or whenever I find the poop bags,
my aussie mutt or the source of my scary dog privileges
take off at no great pace

My toes are aching in my shoes before the first corner
The bus stops are still vacant
The sun can still burn the tops of my shoulders

or the crest of my cheeks but it's a small price
to pay for solitude of any kind
When he and I —or her and I walk

we're blue. Electric blue from the accents on my ragged shoes
my to my aussie's harness or the stinking bags swinging
from my two fingers

Blue is not my favorite color
not remotely
but when we make the turn

past the stoplights and the apartment where that yappy pug lives,
the crow in the big oak screams
or cackles or bounces its beady, perylene eyes—

I imagine that it could be
But then I'm home and the mundane magic
of good weather, warm wind and seasonal joy

crashes into my front door frame; scattering
I strip off sweat and the gravel
stuck in the fibers of my socks somehow

I disassemble the weekend and odd luxuries
My favorite color is comfortably purple—yellow
If I'm sure of who or what I am this morning

BRYNN TESKE

Brynn Teske is an LGBTQ+ poet and novelist based in Minnesota. He's an undergraduate with a passion for writing about marginalized voices and mental health awareness. Brynn has been a lifelong writer, writing his first novelette in third grade. His work has appeared in Red Weather Literary Magazine, Firstwriter's online publication, and is forthcoming in PCC Inscape Magazine. Brynn lives and works out of his apartment where he lives with his fiancee. He enjoys caring for their animals and creating digital art.

40. DAWN

With whispers of autumn,
the day begins to rise

The pastel horizon
tells me that
the dawn is coming

Swaying curtains
bring me scent of the new day

'Hello'
The day echoes

YUU IKEDA

Yuu Ikeda is a Japan based poet. She loves writing, drawing, and reading mystery novels. She writes poetry on her website. https://poetryandcoffeedays.wordpress.com/ Her published poems are "On the Bed" in <Nymphs>, "Pressure" in <Selcouth Station Press>, "Dawn" in <Poetry and Covid>, "The Mirror That I Broke" in <vulnerary magazine>, and more. Her Twitter and Instagram : @yuunnnn77

41. SILENCE OF SNOW

so quiet, still
impossible to place -
this lack of
noise without
birdsong
automobile
airplane.
no wind
no howl of hounds,
only this:

a breathless pause
a silence as deep as sleep.

tranquil,
sparkling,
milky blanket
shrouding the earth
and amazing all,
like a step into Narnia.

you pause before
your foot makes an irreversible
crunch.
how long can you wait before
you break the spell
with breath,
with movement?

nature's holy incantation
broken magically by
a cardinal
gracing the white void
landing on a branch of spruce pine.
with an indignant ruffle of feathers, he
reassures himself
of Spring's certain return.

NICOLE FARMER

Nicole Farmer is a writer and teacher living in Asheville, NC. Her poems have been published in The Closed Eye Open, The Sheepshead Review, The Roadrunner Review, East by Northeast Lit. Review, Wild Roof Journal, Bacopa Literary Review, West Trade Review, The Great Smokies Review, Kakalak Review, 86 Logic, Wingless Dreamer and others. Her play 50 JOBS was produced in Los Angeles. Nicole has been awarded the First Prize in Prose Poetry from the Bacopa Literary Review, which will appear in Sept. 2021. Way back in the 90's she graduated from The Juilliard School of Drama. You can find her dancing barefoot in her driveway on the full moon at midnight.

42. A LOVE LETTER TO WHAT FOLLOWS

the last few years before higher education
are summer that never ends; bright light
in your eyes and cracked skin like the
soil below your shoes. it is good when it
begins, but I get thirstier as time moves
on, holding my parched, bloody throat
in your hands. the water bottles are empty.

no one wants to move on. but I grew up
in a constant state of mental flux, thoughts
unspooling from the top of my childhood
bed into grainy puddles on the tile floor.
my grandmother wanted me to drink more
water, even then. this is one of the problems
that I have never gotten better at solving.

she says that I should stay hydrated because
she once ended up in the hospital. there was a
wedding in the family, and helping like she always
used to rubbed her raw enough to break.
it was because she's old, the doctors told us.
post-op, she couldn't have water for five hours.
she wants me to so that i will never grow old.

the relation is tentative, but I think of it each
time I forget to pick up a glass during the day.
it is a ritual, like putting your left foot into the pool
before the right. that has a story behind it too:
one summer, two girls who I used to know taught
me to swim by holding my head under water.
I didn't learn. I like to know where my feet are now.

it's a hard thing to know, and I fail often. I scratch
at the tap in the garden when it doesn't close all
the way. I know it needs to be fixed, but the water
goes to the grass, and I am worried that it will

die without it. half the world away, a friend of mine
is at her window. as I tell my mother we need the
electrician, she looks at the sun and waters her plants.

she has a brother, and she thinks he's too young for
his age, because he hosed down his dresser and
ruined the wood. he got water everywhere, flooding
their room. she put her phone on a table so I could
talk to her as she cleaned. her brother could have
washed the dresser with a cloth, but I got to meet her.
and I was happy to see her laugh with wet towels.

I go up to the roof of a nearby building every week.
I don't think I'm allowed, because I don't live there,
but I can see the sunset. through a camera, everything
feels touchable and transient at the same time.
growing up, I didn't know how the beach was so big,
and looking at the sky makes me feel that young again.
it is warm, and I am older. the water bottles are empty.

SYNA MAJUMDER

Syna Majumder loves to write about mocktails, bass lines, and horrible people. If feeling particularly soft, her poems focus on sunshine, beaches, and all her friends. Their work has been published most recently in Catatonic Daughters, Pareodolia Lit and the Augment Review and is forthcoming in the Bitchin' Kitsch and the Global Youth Review, among others. You can find her @fuzz_pedals on Instagram.

43. LONG PRISTINE YARDS ALWAYS AHEAD

The longest yards are in front of us
They reach out pristine
Shorter yards lay soiled behind
Their sharp grass broke us open like a sieve
We've grated slowly, with eyes full of sky and grass
After we've no more to leave
Long pristine yards always ahead
Eyes full

G.L. NEWMAN

G.L. Newman is the token son of a Father and a Mother, the token brother to one alive sister and one dead sister. He's the token spigot of words that seem to come whenever they want and refuse to be seen as they were imagined. He was born into an idyllic life which he has never learned to fully appreciate and will, someday, leave. He's hopeful, though. He's here for now.

44. THE TREES WAKE UP

Daylight creeps over the mountains to settle in the valley, slowly, lazily, stretching like a cat over the fields and homes. The trees wake up, it's time for their moment of glory ; their autumn colors spotlighted in the morning chill.

MARY NEWCOMER

Mary Newcomer was born in the USA, but has lived most of her adult life living the French Alps, enjoying their beauty every day. She writes poetry in English and French. She was recently published twice by Wingless Dreamers. Her French poetry has been published by many French poetry magazines. She has been teaching English to French professional adults for many years and it's a job she likes and that continues to challenge her.

45. PLAYGROUND

I walked to the playground
Many fun things there to do
Climb on the monkey bars
And go on the swings too

Time was passing by me fast
Until I got the cruel insult
The mom asked me to leave
Saying it's not meant for an adult

J.M. ALLEN

J. M. Allen is a 50+ year old, who recently started writing a bunch of rhyming poems. He is a long-time resident of Rochester, Minnesota.

46. IN THE COOL OF THE MORNING

In the cool of the morning
Your beauty
Freshness like the rising sun
The mottling of the shade
Cannot hide your sparkle
Of your smile
Of your eyes
Of the strands of your hair in the sun
To hold your hands
To gently kiss your lips
Holding your hand
Softly
With a gentle caress
Lips touching
Ever so gently
A caress across your cheek
A gorgeous soul
A beautiful woman

ROD FRANCISCO

Rod is writer from sub-tropical Central Queensland who has an avid collection of folders and journals filled with half-finished works, concepts, and ideas. Writing more for personal enjoyment and reflection than anything else, Rod has engaged in a range of different styles in poetry, short stories, and scripts; some of which have been longlisted, shortlisted, and published. Most recently Rod's poems "Jigsaw" and "Can you imagine?" were published in the 2020 Dark Poetry Collection; his poem "Darkness of Sunrise" was published in the 2021 Emily Dickinson Poetry Collection.

47. IF YOU LISTEN...

If you listen,
God speaks,
His voice subtle, yet distinct.
Amidst dawn's hush
He whispers—
the gentle gurgle across the rippling lake,
a snapping twig in the nearby brush,
the rustle of stirring leaves.
His breath casts radiance upon all it touches—
golden reflections dazzling the water's surface,
glowing amber through the pines.
The majesty
fills with awe,
yet cradles in comfort—
all troubles minimized,
insignificant within this vast splendor.

If you wake to such a moment,
privileged to observe the discernments
and experience the voice of God,
you come to know
that He, too, has listened.

CHRISTA PLANKO

Christa Planko, MA, is a professional writer with a passion for creative expression. She has had her poetry and short stories featured in several publications, including River Poets Journal, Tanka and Haiku Journal, Poetry Quarterly, and Every Day Fiction. Recently, her story, "The Olde-Tyme Village," won the 2021 WordCrafter Short Fiction Contest. Christa resides in South Jersey with her 4 feline muses. For her bio and list of published works, visit the website: christascorner.godaddysites.com.

48. RUST

Weathered metal
dulling with time,
defaced by
neglectful hands;
it waits sheltering
hoping for reprieve
where sunlight
displays golden crowns,
only seen in certain lights,
open perspectives.

If rusty skin
flicks away
caressed by falling drops
its skeleton is seen,
stoical, but look to rust:
bronzed-red,
tree-bark brown,
richly decadent
as swirled hot chocolate.

Are people the same?

If we flake away
peeling layers,
perceived surfaces,
we remove prejudice;
tormenting taints;
jaded judgements.

Beneath
an inner steel lurks
buried deep
beyond society's grasp
due to plastic profiles
deflecting truth,

marring quality.

For a rusty crown
is still a crown
even with withered gold
its loops and swirls
draped magisterially,
infringed with jewels
now tarnished:
dirt-coloured, muddied over,
yet once shone,
dazzling as Monroe's

painted red lips,
only fallen from up high,
bleeding grace
as it tumbles,
smashing to rusty shards.

A blood-rust key
leaches worth…
pouring into drains
dispelled, over-trodden,
lost by pavements.
No one sees it wink,
flirting for a better home;
it runs with the tide
of unfeeling leather brogues:
pushed into a drain
where its beauty
remains locked,
held fast to itself
as a truthful lover.

Rust washes downstream
filling oblivion;
marring indefinitely
its golden lustre

and God-like sheen.
I spot metallic monarchs,
lobbying to restore
leaden thrones;
I unpick them clean,
admiring rusty rebellion.

EMMA WELLS

Emma has poetry published with and by: The World's Greatest Anthology, The League of Poets, The Lake, The Beckindale Poetry Journal, Dreich Magazine, Drunken Pen Writing, Porridge Magazine, Visual Verse, Littoral Magazine, The Pangolin Review, Derailleur Press, Giving Room Magazine, Chronogram and for the Ledbury Poetry Festival. She also has published a number of short stories and her first novel, *Shelley's Sisterhood*, is due to be published shortly.

49. ECHOES

Echos from
jigsaw of dream
stream intense roses
closing on eyelids
petals of blood ire
beneath the thorn
then shadow born
new ways torn
from alphabet shorn
in the mirror a twinkling
reawakening for tomorrow
blisters stolen sorrow
the metre stretches out
the day's new guards all shout
as senses rise
in an arc of jeweled desire
beside a lake
beside a fire
igniting flames
beyond your dreams.

CLIVE GRESSWELL

At 63-years-young Clive Gresswell has appeared in many poetry magazines and collections. His latest, a chapbook called 'Strings' is published by erbacce press.

50. A WALK AT DAWN

what is it
about a walk
around the block
at 4 am
after a long
night, having not
been able to
fall asleep.
Cold morning's fresh
air helps sooth
something inside me.
But what is
it, is it
the way light
turns before sunrise
blue, gorgeous.
is it the way
I can still
see the moon
waning.
Getting back
I spot
a robin in
my front yard
dusty wings, reddish
gold belly, hopping
though the clover
in bloom. it's
yellow tipped beak
digs through the
mud for worms
I can't remember
the last time
I saw a robin
in the city.
I can only
think of the

last time I
lived at home
when I saw
robins build a
nest on the
doorway of Dad's
garage. day after
day. I'd always
find the mother
under our rhododendrons.
by the summer
of that year
the young could
fly up & out
above the old
cherry blossom trees.

LUKE THOMAS SILLIMAN

Luke Thomas Silliman was born and raised in the Olympic Peninsula of Washington State, loving to write from an early age Luke has always been captivated by the art of storytelling. Writing short stories, poetry and screen plays. Luke Silliman moved to Chicago in 2017 to pursue a degree in Cinema Arts & Science at Columbia College of Chicago and will graduate in 2022.

51. WE SAW THE FLOWERS YESTERDAY

We saw the flowers yesterday, but you won't remember
Life rests in the here and now
Radiant blooms don't last either
But that doesn't make them less worthy

In those minutes, surrounded by color
We can gently sway, as they do
Walking hand in hand
And you might recognize some familiar patterns in their petals

Stay a while longer; there's more to see
They won't wilt...just yet
We will stay and trace nature's lines and curves together
In this moment we have, right now

JULIE CREASEY

Julie Creasey is a freelance writer in Ottawa, Canada. She's not a gardener, but loves to visit gardens and spend time in nature with her family and two daughters.

52. EARTH MORNING

Darkness crawls away
against approaching sun.
Sky, clouds, birds, trees, air,
hold themselves still for the beginning summons.
A dawn call is seldom left unanswered.
Earth's lungs freeze in mid breath,
then releases in a shuddering exhalation,
shimmering across an awakening world.

DAN FITZGERALD

Dan Fitzgerald lives quietly in Pontiac, Illinois, tending to home and garden. His poems have been published in The Writer's Journal, PKA Advocate, Nomad's Choir and many others. His work is also included in several anthologies.

53. THE GATES OF THE SKY

Red clouds swirl through the fading blue mist
The evening sky erects its gates
The land above opens its doors to all who look
All who see the wonder and beauty
The lush purple slowly blending with the dark but beautiful red
The clouds appear to roll toward the sun as it sets in its nook
Tucked away for the night
Until it shines as the morning light
Leading to a land lest travelled to

LILY ANDERSON

Lily Anderson and is a young and aspiring author who wants to change the world, one reader, at a time. She loves sharing her work with others and the world and she is eager to be published. She has been writing since a young age and is an avid reader. She was recently published with you for the first time in the 12 o'clock poetry contest with her poem titled 'Darkness'.

WRITE. FEEL. PUBLISH

WHO SAID THAT YOU CAN'T BE A DREAMER? WATCH ME DOING IT.

If you liked our work, kindly do give us reviews on Amazon.com/winglessdreamer. It will mean a lot to our editorial team. You can also tag or follow us on social media platforms:

Instagram: @winglessdreamerlit @ruchi_acharya

Facebook: www.facebook.com/winglessdreamer

Mail us: Editor: editor@winglessdreamer.com

Sales: sales@winglessdreamer.com

Website: www.winglessdreamer.com

You can also support our small creative community through donation:

www.paypal.me/Winglessdreamer

WRITE AND WRITE, AND SET YOURSELF FREE.

BOOKS PUBLISHED BY WINGLESS DREAMER

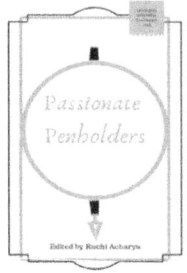  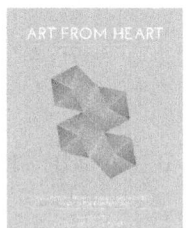

Passionate Penholders   Passionate Penholders II   Art from heart

Daffodils   Father and I   Sunkissed

 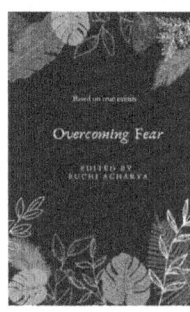 

Tunnel of lost stories   Overcoming Fear   The Rewritten

BOOKS PUBLISHED BY WINGLESS DREAMER

Fruits of our Quarantine   Magic of motivational   Diversity

Dark poetry collection   A glass of wine with Edgar   Heartfelt Poetry

A tribute to Lord Byron   Wicked Young Writers   Snowdrops

BOOKS PUBLISHED BY WINGLESS DREAMER

The Wanderlust Within   Writers of Tomorrow   BIPOC Issue

 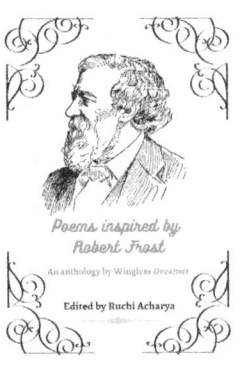 

An evening with Emily Dickinson   Poems inspired by Robert Frost   Shakespeare of today

BOOKS PUBLISHED BY WINGLESS DREAMER

It's time to snuggle up

Depths of Summer

Flee to Spring

How to stay positive

It's twelve o clock

Dreamstones of Summer

Dawn of the day

Made in the USA
Coppell, TX
17 October 2021